Best Wishes,

Martha Turner

D1351142

Money Snacks

A Daybook for Enjoying a Rich Life

Martha Turner

Published by Tell Me About It!, L.L.C.
Atlanta, Georgia
770-936-3035
www.marthascorner.com   •   Martha@marthascorner.com

The information contained in this book is intended to be educational and not to provide personalized legal, accounting, financial or investment advice. This information should not replace consultation when necessary in these areas. The author and publisher are in no way liable for any misuse of the material in this book.

Cover and book design: Jill Dible

Library of Congress Cataloging-in-Publication Data has been applied for.

First Edition
ISBN-13 978-0-9678543-1-1

Printed in Canada

Introduction

You may ask yourself — "What is a Money Snack, and will it make me rich?" I hope it does. A money snack is my way of bringing the prospect of wealth into our minds by popping up little ideas every day; little ideas that are in turn ridiculous, pleasant, intriguing and challenging. Mere notions to tease us into entertaining thoughts such as "Why *can't* I be rich?" or "Maybe I'll get a little more involved with money." I want women to find themselves financially, and begin to feel at ease with the subject, for we are better with money than we think; we're just not giving ourselves enough credit.

That is why I'm on a mission to get women to open up to money and to each other, and begin *talking* about what they know and what they don't know; what they're scared of and what they're excited about, and to stop being embarrassed about money in general. The project is called *Tell Me About It!* because I love to hear women tell me what is going on with them in their lives as they try to cope with an ever increasingly complex world of finance and the day to day issues of money. And because I love to share my journey with women and tell you about what I've been discovering along the way.

On my website, marthascorner.com, women are beginning to engage each other with their questions, ideas, stories and advice. This is the beauty of what women do so well — we support each other and help each other along the way. Sometimes you just want to know you're not the only one.

There was a time when I felt totally alone in my struggle to survive financially. I was a single mother, retired from opera because I was nursing my sick grandmother, but still trying to "keep up with the Joneses." I had no training in money management or investing and I viewed it as a very specialized field for Wall Street experts. Boy was I wrong. I wound up educating myself, which wasn't easy at first, but I stuck with it, and ended up coming to a startling Eureka moment: that investing isn't rocket science and it isn't that hard! Why, a child could do it—wait a minute—I'll teach my child to do it. And so I did. I taught her and then I wrote and taught a fun class at her school on all the various aspects of investing and money management. But let me back up and tell you a little story.

It was 7:00 p.m. on a Monday evening and I was cleaning up the kitchen after dinner. I had decided to plunge into the world of finance to find out how to make it big and take care of my family forever. There was a show on public television called The Nightly Business Report and I thought I'd give it a try. As so often happens when dinner is over and the kitchen is messy, I'm all alone. So I switch on my $20 mini black and white TV set to tune in. I'm going to learn about money! I'm going to be in the know! In the club! Me! Yeah. On comes an attractive, well-dressed man saying, "Good evening, I'm Paul Kangas from Miami." That's the very last bit of English he or anyone else spoke until the very end when he said "This is Paul Kangas wishing all of you the best of good-byes!" No kidding. I literally couldn't understand a word they said. The lingo was so heavy and the topics were beyond reckoning for the mere mortal dishwasher such as me.

They showed stock prices, and though I could read the numbers I completely failed to comprehend their meaning. "Coke is trading at 52," he said. So? Is that good or bad or should I care? And that was the *easy* stuff. Then, there were industry reports, market trends, international exchanges and more. Half an hour later, when Paul signed off, I had the kitchen cleaned and was just mopping up. I was hot and sweaty, I was tired and I was nearly in tears. How could they do this to me? Didn't they know I was trying to become financially aware? What kind of a scam was this?

My pride just wouldn't let me accept defeat. I kept at it with a teeth gritting determination to at least understand what they were talking about. Just to prove that I could listen in. My plan was to take it in by osmosis every night during dishwashing, so every night I would hear Paul say his name, and then later he would sign off, and I would put the mop away and move on. But little by little I started to look at stock prices, and figure out what a market trend was. It took *months*, but I did it. I had immersed myself in websites, papers, books and magazines, and the smoke was clearing. I'll never forgot that night Paul ended his show, wishing me the best of goodbyes, when I realized I had understood every word. It was a good feeling, but nothing could compare to the shock of realizing that this was nothing to be afraid of, and that if I could understand it, *anyone* could.

I know that women have fears and uncertainties about money. I have them too. The trick is to understand that money won't cure those fears. They are aspects of our personality that we can heal so that we won't project them onto money and all of our dealings with it. We heal and help each other by talking and listening, and by taking small steps each day toward financial awakening and empowerment.

A financial empire can't be built overnight, but you can build one over time that fits you and your life, and like me, you can feel very proud over all your small successes. My wish for you is that you can realize your inherent worth and wealth as a person, and then find ways to express yourself and your talents. Making a living by doing what you love is better than winning the lottery, because you know you are doing what you were put here on this earth to do, and you are getting paid for it. What could be better? People are meant to connect with one another so that each person contributes to the needs of others, and then receives back what they need. This is why there is never an end to wealth, because we continue the cycle of rendering help and services to each other.

Learning how money systems work is interesting and not too hard. You may not find balancing your checkbook interesting—neither do I, but it keeps the flow of cash alive. Maybe you've always wanted to invest but were too scared to try, or too put off by the heavy financial jargon. There is help for that at marthascorner.com where you can get the basics translated into everyday language. You can also get suggestions on how to start gradually investing so that you don't worry too much about risk. Add a daily dip into Money Snacks and you'll stay focused without getting overly serious.

Someone said that if money will fix it, it's not a problem. I think that's true, and I would like to see women start to operate freely with their money and gain confidence in what they're doing. It's really a question of attitude and emotion. How we feel about money is so critical to how we deal with it that it's a wonder we don't pay more attention to our negative emotions. We've got to get out of the habit of feeling inferior about handling money.

I want you to have what I have, which is a feeling of ease and of excitement about all the possibilities there are for all of us to learn and get good with money. I also want you to feel the camaraderie and support of other women who are on this same journey. There's no need to feel alone because we're all in this together, which is what makes it so great and so fun. We can help each other, share our triumphs and failures and learn more from each other than we ever dreamed. Believe me, the woman behind you in line at the bank has the same problems you do, and the one seated in the next chair over at the salon is silently wondering if she's the only one who just doesn't get it about money or is worried about how she's going to pay for her haircut.

Money Snacks may not make you a millionaire but it can unlock your mind and heart to discover your inner millionaire, the woman of wealth resting just beneath the surface. Take a journey through this light hearted book with me. You're going to get some practical advice on how to finally face your finances and get organized, plus some saving and investing tips. You'll see some silly stuff, some poignant, and you'll hear people from all walks of life weigh in on money, success and true wealth.

There are quotes from famous people, and from everyday people who have some uncommon wisdom and humor. I love hearing what everyone has to say, so the collection is rather broad. Some quotes gave rise to images in my head, and these I tried to render in little photographs, just to share my own amusement or to enrich an idea.

Anytime you don't see quotation marks, it means that I'm speaking, and it's generally to give you specific advice, or to answer a commonly asked question such as "What is a money market?" or "How do I get started investing in stocks?".

I hope you enjoy Money Snacks as much as I do. I'll admit to still laughing out loud at it, even though it was late at night and I had seen it so many times before. I like to laugh about money because I think if you can laugh at it, you can conquer it. So let's take a fresh look at money and have ourselves a little snack. At the end of the year you will be empowered not just to talk about money but laugh all the way to the bank.

Acknowledgments

I would like to express my love and appreciation to the following people:

Sharon Simpson Joseph for first encouraging me to write and for helping me bring my message to the world.

Robert Joseph for creating my website and designing the book, and for his sincere belief that one day I will be technologically advanced.

Jill Dible for an irresistible cover, Drollene P. Brown for her clarity, and Kristen Fancher for sound guidance.

Julie, who is the reason for it all.

Mia and Bill, Laurie, Bob, Patty and Mike for staying close and keeping the family together.

The Girls Time Group: Tina, Bets, Elyse, Beth and Gilda for being the living embodiment of female support.

Betty Boone, soprano, for teaching me to shine onstage and in my heart.

Rubba Ban and Mattie for giving me family.

Teresa and Katherine for their constancy in friendship.

Members of Just Write Atlanta for soldiering on with me as writers.

Matt for opening my heart and teaching me to never throw in the towel.

And finally, for all the women who are ready for a change.

January

January 1

"Whatever you can do or dream you can,
begin it; boldness has genius and magic in it."
Goethe

January 2

"Every morning I get up and
look through the Forbes list of
the richest people in America.
If I'm not there, I go to work."

Robert Orben

January 3

To create wealth, you must
understand your own
innate value as a person.

January 4

Martha Washington is the only woman on a U.S.
bill: the $1 Silver Certificate.   Go Martha!

January 5

"Each day, and the living of it,
has to be a conscious creation
in which discipline and order
are relieved with some play
and pure foolishness."
Mary Sarton

January 6

"Until you make peace with who you are,
you'll never be content with what you have."
Doris Mortman

January 7

"To be a success
in business,
be daring, be first,
be different."

Unknown

January 8

From the
Give Yourself Credit Department

Women manage the money
and pay the bills in 75% of
all American households!

January 9

"All I ask is the chance to prove that money can't make me happy."   Spike Milligan

January 10

You can dial information for free if you don't mind listening to an ad. I don't mind because it's easier than looking something up, and so handy if you're in the car or away from home. 1-800-373-3411 or 1-800-freeinfo.

January 11

Don't define yourself by what you buy.

January 12

"Money for me has only one sound: liberty."
Coco Chanel

January 13

Take care of yourself and your money, and
then you can take better care of others.

January 14

"Many are called but few get up."
Oliver Herford

January 15

Baby boomers (b. 1946-1964) are saving about 1/3 as much as they will need to maintain their living standards in retirement.

January 16

Now Mama said, "There's only so much money a man really needs, and the rest is just for showing off."   Forrest Gump

January 17

Use the Library!

Get a library card (you're paying taxes for it), and you can order online what you want to have delivered to your local branch: cd's, movies and books. It's free.

January 18

"Money isn't everything as long as you have enough."

Malcolm Forbes

January 19

Invest your $4 daily coffee money at 6%, and in 10 years, after taxes, you've got $15,000!

January 20

"Life is either a daring adventure or nothing. To keep our faces toward change and behave like free spirits in the presence of fate is strength undefeatable."

Helen Keller

January 21

"To take the first step in faith, you don't have to
see the whole staircase: just take the first step."
Martin Luther King, Jr.

January 22

"Money is the symbol of duty,
it is the sacrament of
having done for mankind that
which mankind wanted."

Samuel Butler

January 23

Make sure your spouse has
life insurance, even if you can't
afford very much. At least
$250,000. Make *yourself* the policy
holder, as well as the beneficiary
to avoid probate.

January 24

"The safest way to double your money is to fold it
over and put it in your pocket."   Kin Hubbard

January 25

"Too much of a good thing can be
wonderful."   Mae West

January 26

"There are two things to aim at
in life: first, to get what you want;
and, after that, to enjoy it.
Only the wisest of mankind
achieve the second."

Logan Smith

January 27

"Money doesn't define success
but it makes enjoying it
that much nicer."

Robert Joseph, Ph.D.

January 28

The average
person spends
12 weeks a year
"looking for things."

January 29

"A bargain is something you can't use at a
price you can't resist."   Franklin Jones

January 30

"Don't marry for money; you can
borrow it cheaper."   Unknown

January 31

Stay at home moms, don't undervalue your services as cook, housekeeper, gardener social coordinator, chauffeur, pet sitter, interior designer, tutor, family psychologist, nurse and travel agent.

February

February 1

"The worse the boyfriend, the more stunning your American Express bill."

Wendy Wasserstein

February 2

"Money is the opposite of the weather. Nobody talks about it, but everybody does something about it."

Rebecca Johnson

February 3

From the ***Who Do You Want to Be
When You Grow Up? Department***

"I don't try to be a sex bomb.
I am one."

Kylie Minogue

February 4

Start on your taxes now!

"My mother said, 'You won't amount
to anything because you procrastinate.'
I said 'Just wait.'"

Judy Tenuta

February 5

"Normal is just a cycle on the washing machine."
Whoopi Goldberg

February 6

FALSE ECONOMY

We used to drive old clunkers that always broke down, leaving me stranded and sometimes in danger. But they were paid for! In truth, the constant repairs cost the same as car payments. I coulda had a V8!

February 7

There is no need to judge or
blame yourself for how you
now handle your money.
Try tapping into your native
strengths and developing them.
It doesn't all have to be perfect.

February 8

"In the depth of winter I finally realized that
within me lay an invincible summer."
Unknown

February 9

Take a break from the TV and play Payday, Game of Life or Monopoly. It's a fun way to bring money into the family conversation.

February 10

"How many of us go through our days parched and empty, thirsting after happiness, when we're really standing knee-deep in the river of abundance?"

Sarah Ban Breathnach

February 11

From the
Declutter 15 Minutes a Day Department

"Have nothing in your homes that you do not know to be useful and believe to be beautiful."

William Morris

February 12

"Money talks . . . but all mine ever says is goodbye."   Unknown

February 13

Start Your Taxes Now

Start collecting your tax receipts.
Spend 15 minutes a day gathering
and sorting them. Doing just a little
every day is so much easier than
waiting and having a full-blown
panic attack at the last minute!

February 14

"Love is
the reason
for it all."

Dorothy Fields

February 15

"Remember that not
getting what you
want is sometimes
a wonderful stroke
of luck."

the Dalai Lama

February 16

"By working faithfully eight hours a
day, you may eventually get to be a
boss and work twelve hours a day."

Robert Frost

maybe we should take the road less traveled by . . .

February 17

"We make a living
by what we get.

We make a life by
what we give."

Winston Churchill

February 18

"America... It is a fabulous
country, the only fabulous country;
it is the only place where miracles
not only happen, but where they
happen all the time."

Thomas Wolfe

February 19

"When we change
what we buy ~ and how we
buy it ~ we'll change
who we are."

Faith Popcorn

February 20

"Your head may say this and that, but what
do your feet say? "   Christiane Northrop

February 21

"I felt uplifted, as if I were seeing over the top of a mountain. And to tell the truth, we can handle it: women can breathe the air at these altitudes; we can do the job that needs to be done."

Democrat Nancy Pelosi on becoming the first female whip in the U.S. Congress

February 22

Our word currency stems from the Latin *currere* which is defined as flowing steadily like a current. Keep your money invested and keep it moving.

February 23

"I have never been in a situation where having money made it worse."   Clinton Jones

February 24

Start Your Taxes Now!

Buy your tax software or check in with your accountant this week. Find out what documents are needed to file your taxes. Take this in baby steps.

February 25

PORTFOLIO
not just a hip new downtown bar

This is a list of your
stocks, bonds, mutual funds, CDs,
cookie jar, Money Markets, IRA,
401K, silver buried under the house, savings
accounts & savings bonds.
(I call it my Golden Goose)

February 26

"There will be enough sleeping in the grave."
Benjamin Franklin

February 27

"The only reason I made a commercial for American Express was to pay for my American Express bill."   Peter Ustinov

February 28

Handel was broke when he wrote "Messiah," as many great people have been for some or even all of their lives. You are no more or less your wonderful self, whether you're flush or flat.

February 29

"Though I am grateful for
the blessings of my wealth,
it hasn't changed who I am.
My feet are still on the ground.
I'm just wearing better shoes."

Oprah Winfrey

March

March 1

From the   *Find the Work You Love Dept.*

Warren Buffett, world class billionaire investor, says he's just like you and me; it's just that he "tap dances to work every day" because he *loves* his work.

March 2

Learn to pick your own stocks and make money; click on the *Learning* tab at *marthascorner.com*

March 3

"When women are depressed they either eat or go shopping. Men invade another country."
Elayne Boosler

March 4

The average life span of US bills:

$1	21 months
$5	16 months
$10	18 months
$20	24 months
$50	55 months
$100	89 months

March 5

"Bear in mind that you should conduct yourself in life as at a feast."   Epictetus

March 6

WHAT'S IN YOUR SAFETY DEPOSIT BOX?

will, birth certificates, passports, social security cards, copies of the contents of your wallet, plus insurance policies, mortgages, loans

optional: lock of baby's hair, gold Krugerrands
(in your dreams)

March 7

We all need to earn a certain amount
per year to keep safe and happy,
but when considering career moves,
don't just go for the dough.
Stay within your strengths and your
source of satisfaction.

March 8

"When you have to
make a choice and
don't make it, that is
in itself a choice."

William James

March 9

"I'm a modern woman; most of my fantasies are of more sleep."   Laura Hayden

March 10

Knowing yourself helps you with big purchases like a house or a car. You save big when you *know* you're not keeping up with the Joneses.

March 11

A savings account is a holding tank for money to be used later. It earns interest and builds money up, up, up!

A checking account is a funnel for paying people you owe. It's constant flow makes money go out, out, out!

March 12

"The only way not to think about money is to have a great deal of it."

Edith Wharton

March 13

Understand the difference between stuff & money.
Money has potential ~ stuff is the end.

March 14

"Be who you are
and say what you feel,
because those who
mind don't matter,
and those who
matter don't mind."

Dr. Seuss

March 15

If all the U.S. bills were laid end to end, they would stretch around the earth 24 times.

March 16

"In sixth grade our teacher gave us an aptitude test. She said to me, 'It looks like you could be a telephone operator.' I told my mother, and she said, 'Maybe you should think about being president of the telephone company.'"
Audrey Rice, who sold her software company for 12 million

March 17

"To make a fortune some assistance from fate is essential. Ability alone is insufficient."
Ihara Saikaku

March 18

When asking for a raise, go in knowing you deserve it; visualize getting it, and be prepared to explain the value you add to the company. Know your strengths!

visit *www.salary.com* to find out what others in your field are earning

March 19

Whoa There, Nelly!

Ease up on gifts for coworkers and casual acquaintances if it puts you behind on your bills. Your ego wants to decide how much you can afford, so be aware and don't over-contribute.

March 20

When someone tells you
it's not the money ~ it's the money.

March 21

71% of American teachers say they
have purchased reading materials
for their pupils with their own money
due to lack of books and supplies.

that is so wrong

March 22

"Truth is beautiful, without a doubt.
But so are lies."   Ralph Waldo Emerson

March 23

"And the day came when the risk it took to remain tight in the bud was more painful than the risk it took to blossom."   Anais Nin

March 24

"You can offer so much that costs little or nothing. What you give of yourself is priceless."

Oprah Winfrey

March 25

When stock picking, you're picking a *company*. Remember that. It is *not* a lucky number.

Exercise: Draw the company and what it does with a crayon. If you can't, you don't really understand the company on an intuitive level.

March 26

"Whoever said money can't buy happiness simply didn't know where to go shopping."

Bo Derek

March 27

Money is a powerful symbol of energy;
use it to power you on your way.

March 28

"My father taught me how to work, but not
how to enjoy it."   Abraham Lincoln

March 29

"What's money?
You're a success if you get up in the
morning and go to bed at night and in
between you do what you want to do."

Bob Dylan

March 30

"There is a price to pay for leaving things
as they are."   Unknown

March 31

"To love, health and money. . . and time to enjoy them."   ·   Italian Toast

April

April 1

"When you
come to a
fork in the road,
take it."

Yogi Berra

April 2

FACE YOUR FINANCES!

"The death of fear is in doing
what you fear to do."

Sequichie Comingdeer

April 3

"The purpose of life is to
live it, to taste experience to
the utmost, to reach out eagerly
and without fear for newer and
richer experience."

Eleanor Roosevelt

April 4

"If you think nobody cares about you, try
missing a couple of payments." Unknown

April 5

"I will not be triumphed over."
Cleopatra

April 6

"We don't know
who we are until
we see what we
can do."

Martha Grimes

$ Money Snacks

April 7

I shied away from investing because I couldn't understand all the financial jargon. It took me a year to figure it out, only to realize it didn't mean anything. Since then, I've made pretty good money (but not because I understand big words), so I know you can too.

April 8

Teaching your kids to make money provides for them better than giving them a fortune.

April 9

"He had heard people speak
contemptuously of money:
he wondered if they had ever
tried to do without it."

W. Somerset Maugham

April 10

Everyone is a genius, only on
different subjects.

April 11

"Follow your own path, and let people talk."

Dante

April 12

I lost my IRS refund check for more than $3,000. I was scared and embarrassed to call them, but they were really nice about it. Go figure.

Moral: Sometimes it's better to have the money than to have your pride.

April 13

There's big money in
small things.

The world's most
mass-produced clothing line
was for a Barbie doll.

April 14

"It's better to give than to lend, and it
costs about the same."   Philip Gibbs

April 15

"The hardest thing to understand is the income tax."   Albert Einstein

April 16

"All progress is based upon a universal innate desire on the part of every organism to live beyond its income."
Samuel Butler

hence the birth of the credit card

April 17

"I've got all the money I'll ever need
if I die by four o'clock this afternoon."
Henny Youngman

April 18

Ancient Babylonians inscribed
checks on clay tablets and
used them as their currency
instead of cash.

was that First National Babylonia?

April 19

"Success didn't spoil me;
I've always been insufferable."

Fran Lebowitz

April 20

"Believe that you have it, and you
have it."   Latin Proverb

April 21

"Let how you live stand for
something, no matter how small
and incidental it may seem."

Jodie Foster

April 22

"I'm lazy. At work my favorite part of the
day is being on hold."   Janet Rosen

April 23

LEAVE THAT ALONE!
Don't sneak money from savings and
retirement to buy big kid toys.

April 24

"Happiness does not consist
in things themselves but in the
relish we have of them."

Francois, duc de Rochefoucauld

April 25

"They say it is better to be
poor and happy than rich
and miserable, but how about
a compromise like moderately
rich and just moody?"

Princess Diana

April 26

"Even if you are on the right track, you'll get run
over if you just sit there."   Will Rogers

April 27

"Big girls need big diamonds."
Elizabeth Taylor

April 28

Next time you're shopping, don't just
be a customer. If you love a certain
shop, research it and see if it might be a
good stock to own. We're all doing
field work without knowing it.

April 29

I used to be such a psycho spender
I sometimes had to unload my
trunk in the middle of the night so
my husband wouldn't try asking
me what I was doing with all
those Marshall's bags.

April 30

"Be bold and mighty forces will come
to your aid."　　　Unknown

May

May 1

"Sticking to it
is the genius."

Thomas Edison

May 2

"So what do we do? Anything.
Something. So long as we just
don't sit there. If we screw up,
start over. Try something else.
If we wait until we've satisfied
all the uncertainties, it may
be too late."

Lee Iacocca

May 3

"It's not true that life is one damn thing after another ~ it's the same damn thing over and over."

Edna St. Vincent Millay

May 4

"O snail, climb Mt. Fuji,
But slowly, slowly!"   Issa

May 5

"Laughter is an instant vacation."
Milton Berle

May 6

"A home's tranquility always
comes from within.
The space one's soul requires
cannot be measured in
inches, feet, or dollars."

Sarah Ban Breathnach

May 7

Nessie, the Loch Ness monster,
is protected by the 1912
Protection of Animals Acts
of Scotland.
With good reason.
Nessie is worth up to $40 million
annually to Scottish tourism.

May 8

"Responsibility is the price of freedom."
Elbert Hubbard

May 9

"What my mother believed
about cooking is that
if you worked hard and
prospered, someone else
would do it for you."

Nora Ephron

May 10

If you haven't had one in two years,
ask for a raise!

May 11

"Don't be afraid that your life will end. Be afraid that it will never begin."   Grace Hansen

May 12

Put Me Down For Later . . .

To get your picture on a US bill, you must be known for something you have done for our country and you must be dead.

May 13

"It's a funny thing about life; if you refuse to accept anything but the best, you very often get it."

W. Somerset Maugham

May 14

"If you have money, you are wise and good looking and can sing well too."   Yiddish proverb

May 15

"Nothing will work unless you do."
Maya Angelou

May 16

"**First,** have a definite, clear, practical
ideal ~ a goal, and objective.
Second, have the necessary means
to achieve your ends ~ wisdom,
money, materials and methods.
Third, adjust all your means to that
end."

Aristotle

May 17

You are here for a reason.
There is something only you
can do, in your own way.
Figure it out, even if
it seems to take forever.

May 18

"My life is a bubble;
but how much solid
cash it costs to keep that
bubble floating!"

Logan Smith

May 19

"They always said the women's movement had no sense of humor. Well, we do. It's just that we laugh when the joke's not on us."

Robin Tyler

May 20

"Guilt is the price we pay willingly for doing what we are going to do anyway."

Isabelle Holland

May 21

"Jump."

Joseph Campbell

May 22

"The secret of living is to find
people who will pay you money
to do what you would pay to
do if you had the money."

Sarah Caldwell, opera conductor

May 23

"I want my children to have all
the things I couldn't afford.
Then I want to move in with them."

Phyllis Diller

May 24

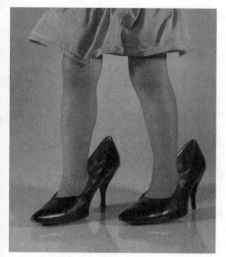

"Lead me not
into temptation;
I can find the
way myself."

Rita Mae Brown

May 25

"In spite of the cost of living,
it's still popular."

Kathleen Norris

May 26

Chotzkah Hall of Shame
Declutter 15 minutes every day!

May 27

If you had 10 billion $1 bills and spent one every second of every day, it would take you 317 years to go broke.

May 28

Does your positive self image depend on your *always* coming through for others, even if it puts you behind on your bills?
Take care of yourself to better take care of others.

May 29

"Do what you can,
with what you have,
where you are."

Unknown

May 30

"You will fail yourself to success."

Unknown

May 31

Acclaimed folk artist Grandma Moses, (Anna Mary Robertson) didn't begin painting until she was 78 because she was too busy making a living farming. It's never too late to follow your dream.

June

June 1

"The only point in making money is, you can tell some big shot where to go."

Humphrey Bogart

June 2

Sometimes a promotion isn't right for you if it takes you away from your native talent and from what you love to do. Is the money really worth it?

June 3

WHERE DOES IT ALL GO?

For the shock of a lifetime, pay with cash only for one week and find out.

not for the faint hearted . . .

June 4

"Compound interest is the most fascinating and powerful force on earth."   Albert Einstein

June 5

Visit *www.autos. msn.com* under Driving Tools. Click on **gas prices** to find the cheapest gas.

June 6

Money used to be made of pure silk.
It's now made of 25% linen and 75% cotton.

June 7

"We love our habits
more than our income,
often more than our life."

Bertrand Russell

June 8

"When a fantasy turns you on, you're
obligated to God and nature to start
doing it ~ right away."   Unknown

June 9

"Ask your child what he wants for dinner
only if he's buying."   Fran Lebowitz

June 10

We Know What She's Talking About . . .

"All of my possessions for
a moment of time."
Elizabeth I

June 11

How much do you owe?

Check out marthascorner.com
and click on *Learning* to calculate
your debt. This isn't to depress you! It's
good to know in round numbers what
you earn vs. what you owe, so
you can keep things in balance.

June 12

"Never spend your money before you have it."
Thomas Jefferson, (who died a debtor)

June 13

"The harder you work, the luckier you get."
Unknown

June 14

"Everything on this earth
has a purpose, and
every person a mission."

Native American Saying

June 15

"Keep a high vitality; keep insured; keep sober; keep cool."   Unknown

June 16

"Remember, bulls make money and bears make money, but pigs get slaughtered."

Unknown

June 17

From the *Why We Like to Feel Good About Money Department*

How you feel about money drives how you deal with it, and determines the decisions you will make with money.

June 18

"If you love someone, set them free.
If they come back, they're probably broke."
Rhonda Dickinson

June 19

When choosing stocks, think long
term ~ 10 to 20 years long.
Find a company you understand,
and that you know will be
in demand for many years to come.

June 20

"Make voyages! Attempt them! There's
nothing else." Tennessee Williams

June 21

"The barrier between you and success is not something that exists in the real world."
Unknown

June 22

People used to save their cash in kitchen jars from *pygg* clay. They became known as piggy banks and were shaped like pigs.

June 23

A brokerage is where you buy
and sell stocks and mutual funds.

visit ***www.marthascorner.com***
and click on ***Learning*** to find
the best rated brokerages.

June 24

"There are people who have money and
people who are rich."   Coco Chanel

June 25

Clutter drowns us.
Clutter up your bank account instead.

June 26

Compound interest is like diamonds
in your backyard. Time will build
wealth for you effortlessly if you'll
just start saving and investing *now*.

June 27

"I have a teenage daughter who wants to go to college. But I wonder why I should pay for her education, when she already knows everything."

Sheila Kay

June 28

The first US silver coins came from Martha Washington's silver service.

June 29

"If there were dreams to sell,
what would you buy?"

Thomas Lovell Bedd

June 30

"Resolve to take fate by the throat and shake
a living out of her."   Louisa May Alcott

July

July 1

You can get a late fee waived
one time on virtually any credit
card. Call the number on the
back of your card and ask to
have the charge removed.
~ not that you'd ever be late ~

July 2

"Money's only
important
when you
don't have
any."

Sting

July 3

"I want a man who's kind and understanding.
Is that too much to ask of a millionaire?"
Zsa Zsa Gabor

July 4

"It was the Fourth of July ~
Independence Day. That holiday
had never meant so much."

Tina Turner, on leaving her
abusive husband, Ike

July 5

"What we must decide is perhaps
how we are valuable rather than
how valuable we are."

Edgar Z. Friedenberg

July 6

"Bad habits are easier to abandon today than
tomorrow."   Yiddish Proverb

July 7

"Like a river, money must keep flowing, otherwise it begins to stagnate, to clog, to suffocate and strangle its very own life force."

Deepak Chopra

July 8

"Money is the seed of money."

Jean Jacques Rousseau

July 9

"Borrow money from pessimists ~
they don't expect it back."

Steven Wright

July 10

"Make visible what, without you, might perhaps
never have been seen."   Robert Bresson

July 11

When it's broiling outside, run fans with your a/c because you'll use less of the costly a/c.

July 12

Sometimes just cleaning what
you have changes everything.
Have you ever shined something
up to sell it, only to realize then
that now you *want* it?

~ maintenance is everything ~

July 13

Talk about money before you get married
so you won't *fight* about it all your lives.

July 14

LOOK BEFORE YOU LEAP!

"Wall Street is an expensive place
to find out who you are."

Unknown

July 15

You can panic over the approach
of swimsuit season, and you can
panic over your high school reunion.
You *cannot* panic when stocks plunge.
You can buy more of a good stock
at bargain prices, but sell only when
you don't think the company can
continue to profit.

July 16

In the early 1900s you could return dirty money to
Washington to be washed and ironed.

July 17

Every day more money is printed for
Monopoly than for the US Treasury.

July 18

"I realized at the age of 61 and a half,
as my mother used to say, ~
'Girl, it's high time you do what
you want to do.'"

Mary Wilson, former Supreme,
on going solo

July 19

SEE THE WORLD

There is about 500 billion dollars
of U.S. currency in circulation
right now, and most of it is held
outside the United States!

July 20

Our clutter has emotional ties. Let go of one
thing a day so you can leave the past behind.

July 21

Start investing for your children NOW! Time is on their side with compound interest.

July 22

It's always the right time to buy a good stock

"In times like these, it's important to remember that there have always been times like these."

Admiral William Crowe

July 23

Now that school schedules have
changed, "off season" for
vacation rentals has changed,
and is earlier. Look for better
rates towards the end of August.

July 24

"We must travel in the direction of our fear."
John Berryman

July 25

"Saving is a
wonderful thing,
especially when
one's parents have
done it for you."

Winston Churchill

July 26

Clear out a closet shelf and keep
gifts there for last minute giving
to teachers, for hostess gifts and
thank-you's. When you see a bargain,
buy it and stash it on the gift shelf.
Buy gift bags at the dollar store.

p.s.   If you are a re-gifter, put a post-it on the
original so it won't circle back home!

July 27

Even if you don't like using a credit card, you need to own one in your own name to establish credit. Find one with no annual fee and a low rate. Use it a bit every month and pay the entire balance every month, on time. Now you'll have credentials when you need a loan, rent a car, make reservations, and more.

July 28

"Find your play and learn how to play it."
Unknown

July 29

How much is enough? they asked John D.
Rockefeller. He replied "Just a little more."

July 30

When I was growing up, it was
vulgar and tacky to talk about money.
Of course you could talk about other
people and their money ~ especially
relatives. Too bad, because nothing
could be tackier than being ignorant
about the power of money.

July 31

Talk About It!

It is said that money is the top reason for divorce today. Make time once a week to check in briefly with your spousal unit on money matters. It's so worth it.

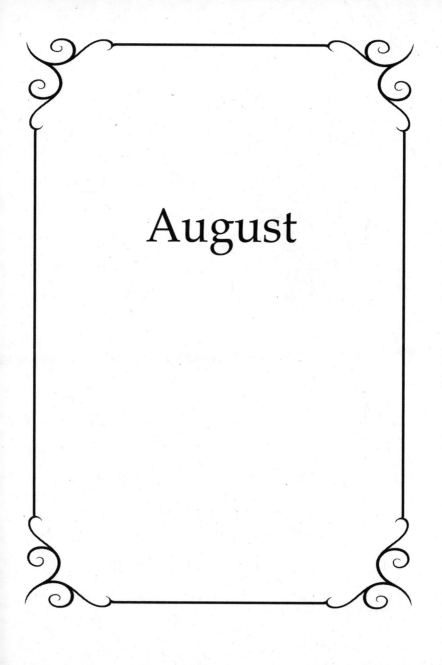

August

August 1

"Never grow a
wishbone, daughter,
where your
backbone ought
to be."

Clementine
Paddleford

August 2

I used to be a landlord because
it was such a great source of
income. The problem was
I hated being a landlord.
So I quit, and my income
is just fine, and so am I.

August 3

Beware of
seeing yourself
as poor ~ for
you may attract
poverty.

August 4

"To get profit without risk,
experience without danger,
and reward without work
is as impossible as it is to
live without being born."

A. P. Gouthey

August 5

"I walk slowly, but I never walk backward."
Abraham Lincoln

August 6

"When I became a stay-at-home dad, it
dawned on me that this is a hard job!
It really sank in what women have been
doing for countless generations with not
a lot of appreciation or support. It's about
10 times harder than I thought it was going
to be. And about 1,000 times greater
than I could have imagined.
Bill Maloney, married to Christine Ebersole

August 7

"Anything that is
of value
in life only
multiplies
when it is given."

Deepak Chopra

August 8

"Three things have helped me
successfully go through the
ordeals of life: an understanding
husband, a good analyst, and
millions of dollars."

Mary Tyler Moore

August 9

What's in a FICO?

Do you know your FICO score?
It's a 3-digit number based on your
credit report, and the higher the
better. Find it for free at
*www.annualcreditreport.com and go to
marthascorner.com to learn more.*

August 10

"There is but one
success ~ to be able
to spend your life in
your own way."

Christopher Marley

August 11

"A man of courage never needs weapons, but he may need bail."   Ethel Watts Mumford

August 12

To show your kids where the money goes, get Monopoly money and count out the monthly family income. Dump it on the kitchen table, then remove the sum for each monthly bill and for savings. When they see what's left over, they'll understand why they can't buy everything, and why their allowance isn't $250 a week, even when they say please.

August 13

Americans spent 1 in 7 of their take-home dollars on paying debt last year, up from 1 in 9 in 1980. Experts say few consumers are even able to calculate the true costs of such payments.

August 14

CLUTTER SWEEP

Pick one room of your house, and remove every bit of clutter and decorative item. Then put back only a third of it. It's a like a breath of fresh air, and you may find you like living with less.

August 15

A group of students introduced
the Liberty Dollar Bill Act
to Congress; it has a short
version of the US Constitution
printed on the back.

. . . good idea

August 16

Eating at home saves big money, and it's
healthier than fast food; *savingdinner.com*
can help make cooking easier.

August 17

"Life is just a mirror, and what you
see out there, you must first see inside
of you."   Wally "Famous" Amos

August 18

"I've never seen a Brink's truck
follow a hearse to the cemetery."

Barbara Hutton,
      Woolworth's heiress

August 19

Don't look for
others to take
care of you.
That's *your* job,
and you can
do it.

August 20

Use a Money Market for your
savings account. It's safe, and you
get a better rate of interest.

www.bankrate.com will give you the
best options for money markets

August 21

"There's one way to find out if a man is honest ~ ask him. If he says *yes*, you know he's a crook."

Groucho Marx

August 22

In the US the $20 bill is the most counterfeited, followed by $100, $10, $50, $1, & $5. The $100 is the most faked abroad.

August 23

"Whether or not it is clear to you, no doubt
the universe is unfolding as it should."
Max Ehrmann

August 24

Sometimes you need a professional
to help you declutter, and the
National Association of Professional
Organizers can help. Go to
www.napo.net and find your state.
Members are listed there, as
are organizing tips. If you pay for
advice, you usually take it.

August 25

"Don't fall in love with your stocks."
Peter Lynch

August 26

"Money should never be turned
into a currency to
purchase self-esteem."

Shmuley Boteach
(Shalom in the Home)

August 27

Break the spell advertising has on your mind. Decide for yourself how best to use your money. You're a person, not a consumer.

August 28

If your dog eats your $20 bill but spits out 51% of it, Washington will replace it free for you.

August 29

From the   *Teach Your Children*
                      Well Department

"If you can't be a good example,
then you'll just have to be
a horrible warning."

Catherine Aird

August 30

"I just hate not having fun."

Kevin Kline,

on being asked how he always
manages to perform with joy.

August 31

Free! Teresa's Tips at *marthascorner.com* lists free stuff from a world class bargain hunter.

September

September 1

"When faced with a decision, I always ask,
"What would be the most fun?"
Peggy Walker

September 2

Don't worry about canceling credit
cards that you aren't going to use
anymore. Right now, Fico scores
are based on how much *unused*
credit you have, so keep 'em open!

September 3

Many people think money decisions
must be made by reason alone.
This is wrong. Use your heart,
and listen for signals in yourself.
You'll be guided by a more
complete accounting system.

September 4

Money is a
go machine.

September 5

"Money isn't everything ~ but it ranks right up there with oxygen."   Rita Davenport

September 6

If you're wondering if you're qualified to start up your own business idea, don't worry! Lots of successful entrepreneurs weren't qualified on paper, like Atlanta's Sara Blakely, inventor of the fabulous Spanx undergarments for women.

September 7

"The trick is in what one emphasizes.
We either make ourselves miserable,
or we make ourselves happy.
The amount of work is the same."

Carlos Castaneda

September 8

"Celebrate what you want to see more of."
Tom Peters

September 9

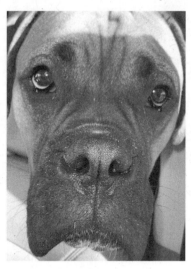

"The minute you
settle for less than
you deserve, you get
even less than
you settled for."

Maureen Dowd

September 10

A Mutual Fund is an investment
made up of several stocks
chosen by a stock picker,
grandly called a "fund manager."

visit *www.marthascorner.com* and click on
the Learning tab to find out more

September 11

"There is enough
in the world for
everyone to have
plenty, to live on
happily and to
be at peace with
his neighbors."

Harry S. Truman

September 12

"If you empty your purse into your
head, no one can take it away from you.
An investment of knowledge always
pays the best interest."

Benjamin Franklin

September 13

"Reality is the leading cause of stress for
those in touch with it."   Jane Wagner

September 14

"It is common sense to take
a method and try it; if it fails,
admit it frankly and try another.
But above all try something."

Franklin D. Roosevelt

September 15

"If you want to say it with flowers,
a single rose says: I'm cheap!"

Delta Burke

September 16

"Seize the moment before it's gone,
For another day begins at dawn."
Clay Harrison

September 17

"You get a real sense of mastery when you are taming the tiger."   Phil McGraw, on debt

September 18

Women can outlive men, so
do make sure you and your
spouse have a will, life insurance,
a durable power of attorney
and a living will.

visit *www.marthascorner.com* for details

September 19

From the
Is It Time For a Raise? Department

Nearly 50% of all
bank robberies
take place on Friday.

September 20

You yourself are a bundle of riches,
waiting to be let out and developed.
Know yourself ~ know your talents.

September 21

Famed billionaire investor Warren Buffett was rejected by the Harvard Business School.

Moral: If you're not failing from time to time you're not risking enough, and you'll miss all the adventure.

September 22

"Children are like paparazzi. They follow you everywhere you don't want them to go, and they take pictures!"

Jamie Lee Curtis

September 23

"If you look good
and dress well,
you don't need
a purpose in life."

Robert Pante

September 24

Don't use your credit card to get cash.
There is always a fee attached, not to
mention interest rates that may be
higher than the rate on your card.

Better: Use an ATM machine that doesn't
charge you any user fee.

September 25

When dining out, go for lunch if you can. You get the same great ambiance and food for a much better price, not to mention the lunch specials.

September 26

BE A PLAYA

Try your hand on the stock market risk free! Sign up to play a free, real time stock simulator game. Everything is real except the money.

visit *www.marthascorner.com* and click on the *Learning* tab to find out where to play

September 27

Money is a symbol of energy.
It gets things done, adds glitter,
supports and protects.
It does not, however,
feed the soul.

September 28

Photocopy everything in your wallet, front
and back and keep it on file. If your purse
gets stolen, you'll have all your info handy.

September 29

From the *Declutter Your Life Department*

Rotate decorative items at home.
You don't have to display everything
you own, and when you notice certain
things are not being called back for
an encore, it's time to let them go.

September 30

I used to buy all this stuff for the
fantasy value ~ an ice cream maker,
a French coffee press, demitasse cups.
I never used any of it, and I'm still
mystified by why I did that.

October

October 1

Money is neutral; you color it with your own personality. If you're fearful as a person, you will be with money as well. If you're optimistic, you will be confident and optimistic in your handling of money.

October 2

"Learn the rules so you know how to break them properly."

the Dalai Lama

October 3

"To be satisfied with
little is hard,
to be satisfied with
a lot is impossible."

Marie von
Ebner-Eschenbach

October 4

DREAM

If you had all the money you would ever need,
had bought everything you wanted and
had traveled everywhere, what would you do
then? List it out, and do it fast. Don't think too
hard because this should come from the gut.
You can really get to know yourself this way.

Have your kids do this too. They'll amaze you.

October 5

Spending more money on wardrobe basics can save money when you see how much wear you get out of them, plus it's great to have clothes that make you feel fabulous. For the trendy, buy small accessories since they'll be gone by next year.

** *Tim Gunn's style guide book includes 10 essentials for women.*

October 6

I used to be so busy accumulating things, there was no time left for enjoying them. It's as though the American Dream became the American Drag.

October 7

"Don't depend on a rabbit's foot for luck.
It didn't do much for the rabbit." Unknown

October 8

Kids need practice with credit cards,
so when they're 18 or so, let them
get one with a low limit, and teach
them to pay it off on time and in full
every month. This is how they'll learn,
and when they succeed in doing this,
allow incremental limit increases.

October 9

"For every difficult question there's a simple answer ~ and it's wrong."

H. L. Mencken

October 10

"Just one great idea can completely revolutionize your life."

Earl Nightingale

October 11

"I divide my bills into
three categories:
late bills;
late, late, bills; and
'Would you buy my kidney?' bills."

Margot Black

October 12

"Life is like a ten-speed bike. Most of us
have gears we never use."   Charles Schulz

October 13

"Don't take
new risks to retrieve
old losses."

Unknown

October 14

Before I was divorced, I didn't feel I
could manage on my own financially.
Imagine my surprise when it was
actually easier on my own. Turns out
I already had it in me to take care of
business, as my friends had told me;
I just didn't believe it.

October 15

"You've got to take the initiative and play your game. Confidence makes the difference."   Chris Evert

October 16

"People think that at the top there isn't much room. They tend to think of it as an Everest. My message is that there is tons of room at the top."

Margaret Thatcher

October 17

I used to be so intimidated by the other women in my daughter's preschool. They were perfect and everything was so perfect in their Rich and Perfect World. Only later did I realize I was having way more fun than they were.

October 18

I put all my bills in a wood tray; otherwise they take wing and fly all over the place.

October 19

Only volunteer for what you *want* to do.

Tip: When asked to help out, ask yourself
"Would I enjoy doing that right now?"
If you answer no now, it'll be no later.
Trust me.

October 20

"She was this fake rich person."
Cayla Brestel

October 21

www.dressforsuccess.org
helps disadvantaged women
enter the workforce and build a career.
After decluttering your closet,
give them a call and lend a
woman a hand.

October 22

"Don't try to
impress others. Let
them have the fun
of impressing you."

Unknown

October 23

SHOPPING RULES

Do I love it?
  Do I need it?
    Do I have a place to put it?
    Can I afford it?

If the answer is yes to all, buy away!

October 24

What is the design on the back of the Arkansas quarter? A diamond: it's the only state in the Union with diamond mines.

October 25

"We are always asking ourselves,
'How am I of value?
What is my worth?' Yet I believe
that worthiness is our birthright."

Oprah Winfrey

October 26

Believe me ~
     it's not about the money.

October 27

"Stop a bad account at once."

Unknown

October 28

"History is always repeating
itself, but each time the
price goes up."

Unknown

October 29

"The phrase 'working mother' is redundant."   Jane Sellman

October 30

Learn to read your bank statement and balance your checkbook. Online bank services are a great time saver if you are comfortable on the computer.

October 31

"The proverb warns that, 'You should not bite the hand that feeds you.' But maybe you should, if it prevents you from feeding yourself."

Thomas S. Szasz

November

November 1

If you're a fashion diva, have
you ever considered helping other
women look as fabulous as you?
This is an age of service industries:
consultants, fashion gurus and
personal shoppers are *in*.

November 2

"What we play is life."
Louis Armstrong

November 3

"Works well when under constant
supervision and cornered like
a rat in a trap."

Actual Manager's Evaluation of an Employee

November 4

"Choose a job you love, and you will never
have to work a day in your life."
Confucius

November 5

"It takes courage to grow up and turn out
to be who you really are."   e.e. cummings

November 6

From the *Face Your Finances Department*

"The truth will set you free.
But first it will piss you off."

Gloria Steinem

November 7

FOR BUDGET HATERS

1. Direct deposit your paycheck.
2. Auto invest in savings.
3. Auto pay bills online, or set up a schedule of what's due and when.
4. Freely spend the leftovers.

November 8

Working really hard in the wrong job is like putting lipstick on a pig.

November 9

INVEST

Don't let the word scare you.
You can go totally risk free with a
Money Market, Savings Bond,
CD or Treasury Note

visit: *www.marthascorner.com* for details

November 10

Document your
achievements
at work, and make
sure your boss
is aware of them.
Women very
often contribute far
more than their
employers realize.

November 11

"Instant gratification takes too long."
Carrie Fisher

November 12

Start your holiday gift list now, and set limits. Remember, the greatest gifts you can give are love and appreciation, so don't feel pressured to overspend on friends and family just to prove you love them.

November 13

"Whatever wrinkles I got, I enjoyed getting them."   Ava Gardner

November 14

Enjoy your money in your own way.
Don't worry that it's not trendy,
chic, cool or even popular;
it just needs to ring your bell.

November 15

Next time someone dismisses you for being a stay-at-home parent, mention that your job lists at *salary.com* for $134,121. I think that's low, and I've heard higher. I wonder what the children would say?

November 16

"If you find a passion you will find a way."
Unknown

November 17

401K

"Plan ahead ~ it wasn't raining when
Noah built the ark."
                              Unknown

November 18

Kids *watch* you, so live within your means,
and they will learn to as well.

November 19

BLING

"You can convert your style into riches."
Quentin Crisp

November 20

"It's a sad day when you find out
it's not accident or time or
fortune, but just yourself that
kept things from you."

Lillian Hellman

November 21

"I always wanted
to be somebody,
but I should have
been more specific."

Lily Tomlin

November 22

Get a credit card in your own
name, and not just so you can
buy more shoes! You need
independent means of support
to provide you with necessary
options. Be prepared for the
winds of fate, for they will blow.

November 23

When you give to a charity, make sure it is soul-stirring and brings you joy when you contribute, because what comes back to you is the same energy you send out, only compounded.

November 24

"Delusions of grandeur make me feel a lot better about myself."   Jane Wagner

November 25

You make the most money when you help other people get what they want. Do what you love to do, but figure out a way to help other people by doing it.

November 26

"It is far easier to be wise for others than to be so for oneself."

duc de
La Rochefoucauld

November 27

"If you knew what I know about the power of giving, you would not let a single meal pass without sharing it in some way."   Buddha

November 28

Save a Little

Some credit cards let you round up each purchase to the next dollar, and they deposit the change into your savings.

November 29

Managing money is about doing a little every day, not about being brilliant or good with numbers.

November 30

When you feel confident and secure as a person, you will begin to deal confidently and securely with your money.

December

December 1

"I like work; it fascinates me; I can sit and
look at it for hours."   Jerome K. Jerome

December 2

Ask me no questions and I'll
tell you no lies. For you and your
spousal unit, a separate splurge
account is a must, for we all need
to do some spending without
having to answer for it.

December 3

"The main reason Santa is so jolly is because he knows where all the bad girls live."

Unknown

December 4

"The difference between try and triumph is a little umph."   Unknown

December 5

"Keep down expenses, but don't be stingy."
Unknown

December 6

You can make a lot of money problems
self-correct by finding balance in your
life and celebrating your strengths. Me,
I'm not good with numbers. So what?
I count on my fingers, use a calculator,
and hire an accountant. It's better to just
do damage control on your weaknesses
and then enjoy your talents.

December 7

"It is everyone's obligation to
put back into the world
at least the equivalent of
what they take out of it."

Albert Einstein

December 8

"The smallest good deed is better than the
grandest good intention."   Duguet

December 9

Money isn't stagnate. Don't ever forget that. It's meant to be moving because it symbolizes energy.

December 10

Failure is just part of the game. Factor it in and don't overreact when something fails. Attempts may fail, but you are not a failure.

December 11

"Unhappiness is in
not knowing what we want and
killing ourselves to get it."

Don Herold

December 12

"You might as
well fall flat on
your face
as lean over
too far backwards."

James Thurber

December 13

Wanting money isn't a sign of greed. When you provide what the world needs, you deserve to be rewarded. Money is always about give and take.

December 14

Clues to Finding Your Strengths

~ Do you lose track of time when you're engaged in this activity?
~ Do you learn it quickly?
~ Would you do this if you had all the time and money in the world?
~ Do you feel strong and authentic when you do this?

December 15

"Then give to the world
the best you have, and the
best will come back to you."

Madeline Bridges

December 16

"A dead end street is a good place to
turn around."   Naomi Judd

December 17

"Angels fly because they take themselves lightly."   G. K. Chesterton

December 18

From the *Extreme Gift Giving Department*

"When it's all over, people look around and say 'What happened?' It's like they have a holiday hangover."

Matthew Fountain

December 19

Believe it or not, money is here to serve and support you; *not* vice-versa.

December 20

What makes the holidays rich is the time we spend just being with the people we love. Money makes it nicer, but you don't need a lot of it to have a really good time together.

December 21

"I've learned that whenever I decide something with an open heart, I usually make the right decision."   Maya Angelou

December 22

Clutter Control!

"You can't have everything. Where would you put it?"
Ann Landers

December 23

"Observe how all things are continually
being born of change ~
Whatever is, is in some sense the seed
of what is to emerge from it."

Marcus Aurelius

December 24

Barush Bashan

"The blessings
already are."

Jewish blessing

December 25

"In our willingness to give that which
we seek, we keep the abundance
of the universe circulating in our lives."

Deepak Chopra

December 26

"The way is not in the sky.
The way is in the heart."   Unknown

December 27

"There is a time for departure even when
there's no certain place to go."
Tennessee Williams

December 28

"Most of us are embedded in our
current language of reality. So inevitably,
we envision a future that comes from the
drift of words wholly based in the past.
We look to the future and ask 'why?'
when we could dream of things that
never were and ask 'why not?'"

Elliott Galloway

December 29

"I am having an out-of-money experience."
Unknown

December 30

"Learn to value yourself, which means:
to fight for your happiness."

Ayn Rand

December 31

Excelsior!
    (Latin for upward and onward)